Celebrations in My World

LABOR DAY

Robert Walker

UAW Kids March
Our Future Depends on it!
Local 7

UNIONS MARCH
UNIONS VOTE

Crabtree Publishing Company

www.crabtreebooks.com

Crabtree Publishing Company

www.crabtreebooks.com

Author: Robert Walker
Series and project editor: Susan LaBella
Editor: Adrianna Morganelli
Proofreader: Reagan Miller
Photo research: Crystal Sikkens
Editorial director: Kathy Middleton
Design: Katherine Berti
Ravinder Kumar (Q2AMEDIA)
**Production coordinator and
Prepress technician:** Katherine Berti

Photographs:
Alamy: Jim West: cover, page 1; Richard Levine: page 10;
Clarke Conde: pages 13, 23, 30
Associated Press: page 25
BigStockPhoto: page 12
Creative Comments: page 19
Dreamstime: pages 5 (calendar), 11, 20, 21, 26, 28
iStockPhoto: pages 5 (inset), 31
Shutterstock: pages 4, 6, 7, 8, 9, 14, 15, 17, 18, 22,
24, 27, 29
Wikipedia: U.S. Department of Labor: page 16

Library and Archives Canada Cataloguing in Publication

Walker, Robert, 1980-
Labor Day / Robert Walker.

(Celebrations in my world)
Includes index.
Issued also in an electronic format.
ISBN 978-0-7787-4929-5 (bound).--ISBN 978-0-7787-4936-3 (pbk.)

1. Labor Day--Juvenile literature. I. Title. II. Series:
Celebrations in my world

HD7791.W34 2010   j394.264   C2010-902755-8

Library of Congress Cataloging-in-Publication Data

Walker, Robert, 1980-
Labor Day / Robert Walker.
p. cm. -- (Celebrations in my world)
Includes index.
ISBN 978-0-7787-4936-3 (pbk. : alk. paper) -- ISBN 978-0-7787-4929-5
(reinforced library binding : alk. paper) -- ISBN 978-1-4271-9446-6
(electronic (pdf))
1. Labor Day--Juvenile literature. I. Title. II. Series.

HD7791.W35 2011
394.264--dc22
                                                    2010016410

Crabtree Publishing Company

www.crabtreebooks.com   1-800-387-7650

Printed in China/082010/AP20100512

Published in Canada
Crabtree Publishing
616 Welland Ave.
St. Catharines, Ontario
L2M 5V6

Published in the United States
Crabtree Publishing
PMB 59051
350 Fifth Avenue, 59th Floor
New York, New York 10118

Published in the United Kingdom
Crabtree Publishing
Maritime House
Basin Road North, Hove
BN41 1WR

Published in Australia
Crabtree Publishing
386 Mt. Alexander Rd.
Ascot Vale (Melbourne)
VIC 3032

Contents

What Is Labor Day?

Labor Day is an **annual** holiday that celebrates workers in North America. Events are held to mark the occasion in different cities.

● Workers play a very important part in our lives.

DID YOU KNOW?

Labor unions are groups of workers who try to make life better for themselves. The first labor union in the United States was formed in 1833.

In the United States and Canada, Labor Day is held on the first Monday in the month of September every year. Labor Day is a holiday, which means that most people do not have to work.

Instead, they are free to enjoy Labor Day any way they choose. A lot of people spend the day watching parades or having a picnic with friends and family.

Look for the first Monday in September to find Labor Day.

September   2010

SUNDAY	MONDAY	TUESDAY	WEDNESDAY	THURSDAY	FRIDAY	SATURDAY
			1	2	3	4
5	⑥	7	8	9	10	11
12	13	14	15	16	17	18
19	20	21	22	23	24	25
26	27	28	29	30		

Celebrating the Workers

A worker is someone who works at a job. Workers are the men and women who help improve our communities. These people can be doctors, lawyers, barbers, or teachers.

- Doctors help keep us healthy.

DID YOU KNOW?

Before there were factories and other big businesses, most people had to make their own clothes and grow their own food.

Workers build the cars we drive.

Many workers have jobs that you might not think about. These men and women work with metals, **fabrics**, and many other things we use every day.

Workers make the clothes you wear, the food you eat, and the books you read. They also make the televisions and computers that you use each day. Labor Day helps us show appreciation for workers.

The First Labor Day

The very first Labor Day celebration in the U.S. was held in New York City on September 5, 1882. Union workers were given the day off from work.

The Labor Day parade has been a tradition in New York City since 1882.

DID YOU KNOW?

American labor leader Peter McGuire organized the first parade in New York after attending a similar parade held in Toronto, Canada.

There were marches, protests, and a huge picnic. The workers were celebrating the improvements made to worker rights, as well as reminding people that more had to be done.

The idea for Labor Day soon spread to other cities, and similar celebrations were held each year across the U.S. and Canada. Labor Day became so popular that in 1894, U.S. president Grover Cleveland finally declared Labor Day a national holiday.

● Former President Grover Cleveland appeared on the last U.S. one-thousand-dollar bill.

Labor Day Parades

Labor Day weekend marks the end of summer for people in North America. With weather in most places still sunny and warm, outdoor parades are a large part of Labor Day celebrations.

Schools sometimes participate in Labor Day parades.

DID YOU KNOW?

Before labor unions were formed, workers who complained about working conditions could lose their jobs.

Riding on floats in a Labor Day parade is fun for the whole family.

Floats and marching bands are often part of the parades for the crowds to enjoy. These parades help celebrate workers, and are a fun event for families to enjoy, too.

Many labor unions take part in Labor Day parades. Thousands of workers will join in the march, along with the floats and marching bands.

Labor Day Events

A lot of people celebrate the holiday by having picnics and barbecues with friends and family.

- A family picnic is a popular Labor Day activity.

DID YOU KNOW?

In the past, workers were not allowed to strike. Often, the police were called in to break up the protests. Many workers were hurt or killed.

14

Fireworks, concerts, and other events are also popular during Labor Day. Most families take the opportunity of a long weekend to travel before a new school year begins.

Beaches, cottages, and amusement parks can get very busy during Labor Day weekend.

People often go camping on the Labor Day long weekend.

More Than a Holiday

The meaning of Labor Day is much more than just an extra day off for people. It celebrates the struggle by workers to improve their rights.

- U.S. Secretary of Labor, Hilda Solis

DID YOU KNOW?

*The Labor Hall of Fame was founded in 1988 to honor the men and women who have worked in the **labor movement**.*

16

Speeches and **demonstrations** by labor leaders and other important people help remind us of the need for improving working conditions.

The U.S. Department of Labor makes great efforts to recognize and celebrate the importance of Labor Day. The **Secretary** of Labor will often give a speech for Labor Day, talking about the accomplishments of the labor movement.

• U.S. Secretary of Labor, Hilda Solis, gives a speech in Los Angeles, California.

Labor Day Symbols

Flags, streamers, and banners are all a part of Labor Day celebrations. It is a time of **patriotism** and of showing appreciation for workers.

Sparklers are popular on Labor Day.

DID YOU KNOW?

*Some people argue that it was not Peter McGuire who first came up with the idea for Labor Day, but a **machinist** named Matthew Maguire.*

18

The U.S. Department of Labor and other labor unions annually make posters for the event. The posters help remind people of the holiday, and let people know where different events are being held.

Many people will decorate their homes as well as themselves for Labor Day. Posters can also be seen on Labor Day. They are put up in store windows and other public places.

Children dress up and ride their bikes in parades.

Around the World

Other countries around the world also have a special day to celebrate their workers. This day is called International Workers' Day.

These people are celebrating May Day in Russia.

DID YOU KNOW?

In many countries, International Workers' Day is also known as "May Day," because it falls on the first day of May.

This event is similar to Labor Day, and is held on the first of May each year. International Workers' Day has roots in the United States.

On May 1, 1886, several protesting workers in Chicago were killed by police who were trying to break up the protest. This day helps people remember those who died. The holiday has since spread to other countries.

Dancers perform during the International Workers' Day celebration in Poland.

Honoring a Holiday

On Labor Day, people can show their appreciation for workers in many ways. In 1956, the United States Postal Service made the first Labor Day **commemorative** stamp. Some people have also written songs and poems to celebrate the event.

- The U.S. Labor Day commemorative stamp

New Zealand holds its own Labor Day on the fourth Monday of October each year.

These people are wearing Labor Day t-shirts to a parade.

Every Labor Day, people often wear new and colorful pins. People will also wear Labor Day t-shirts and hats to a parade.

Many books have been written about Labor Day. There have even been **documentaries** made about the holiday.

Labor Day Organizations

The Department of Labor in the U.S. and the Ministry of Human Resources and Social Development in Canada work to ensure the safety and fair treatment of workers.

The U.S. Department of Labor building in Washington, D.C.

DID YOU KNOW?
Departments of Labor were created in 1900 in Canada and 1913 in the U.S.

24

This includes aiming for better working conditions, **benefits**, and career opportunities for workers.

Each department assists workers in need. Many different jobs and **trades** have their own unions. There are unions for teachers, truck drivers, and electricians. These unions help workers protect their rights and interests.

Union members meet regularly to talk about labor issues.

Labor Today

The working conditions for people today have greatly improved thanks to the help of worker unions and groups. Most workers are paid a fair **wage**, and do not have to do jobs that are unfair or dangerous.

- Factories are no longer the dangerous workplaces they used to be.

DID YOU KNOW?

In the past, many workers were forced to work for almost 16 hours a day. Today, many workers enjoy an eight-hour workday.

Demonstrations, such as the one shown below, have helped workers get the treatment and support they deserve.

Limits have also been placed on how many hours a day a person must work. Unions have been powerful in getting workers the rights and safety they deserve.

Factories, mines, and other formerly dangerous places to work are now much safer. Governments have even passed laws and regulations to protect worker rights.

27

Labor Day in Schools

Although Labor Day takes place before the start of the school year, many schools have events and activities to recognize the holiday.

Schools make sure to teach students about the importance of Labor Day.

DID YOU KNOW?

The American Federation of Labor and Congress of Industrial Organizations is the largest group of labor unions in the United States. There are over 11 million members.

Workers and union officials are invited to speak to students about Labor Day. It is important for students to understand the story of labor.

Students learn about the struggles and improvements made to the conditions and pay for workers. The labor movement is a very important part of our history.

There are plenty of books in your school library about Labor Day.

Get Involved!

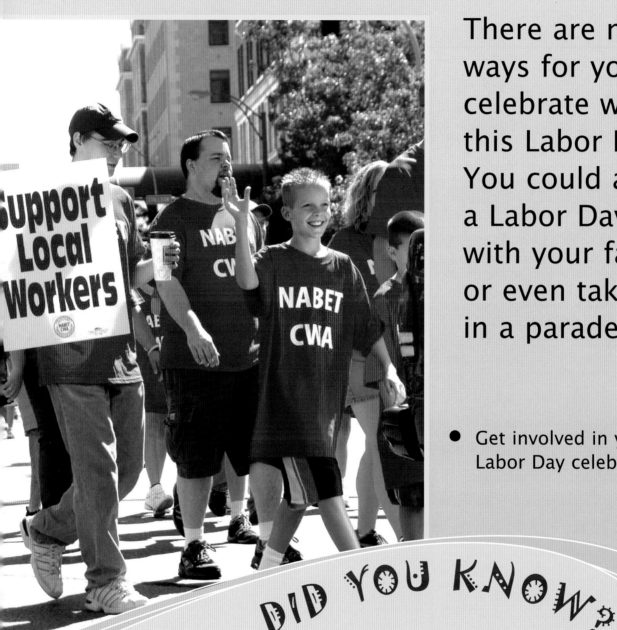

There are many ways for you to celebrate workers this Labor Day. You could attend a Labor Day event with your family, or even take part in a parade.

- Get involved in your local Labor Day celebrations.

DID YOU KNOW?

Even the actors who appear in movies and television shows have unions. They are the Screen Actors Guild (SAG) and the Alliance of Canadian Cinema, Television, and Radio Artists (ACTRA).

Thank your teacher on Labor Day for the work she or he does.

You could even write a letter to a worker that you know, saying thank you for the work he or she does.

You and your friends might want to try some fun Labor Day games and activities. Just ask your parents or teacher to help you find some ideas. There are plenty of books in your library and a lot of Internet sites you can check out, too.

Glossary

annual Every year

benefits Something extra, such as health insurance, provided by an employer

commemorative Remembering a person, place, or thing

demonstration A public meeting intended to change something

documentary A film that tells the story of something

fabric The cloth used to make clothes

labor movement An organized effort by workers to improve their rights on the job

machinist A person who makes or works on machines

patriotism Being supportive of your country

protest A complaint or display of disapproval

right The fair treatment of a person

secretary A person in charge of a group or organization

strike To stop work in order to force an employer to meet worker demands

trade A job skill

wage Money paid to a person for doing a job

working class People who work in industrial, service, or manual jobs

Index